Backyard Animals
Foxes

Anita Yasuda

www.av2books.com

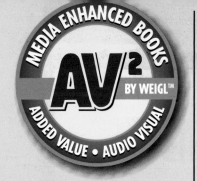

AV² provides enriched content that supplements and complements this book. Weigl's AV² books strive to create inspired learning and engage young minds in a total learning experience.

Your AV² Media Enhanced books come alive with...

Audio
Listen to sections of the book read aloud.

Key Words
Study vocabulary, and complete a matching word activity.

Video
Watch informative video clips.

Quizzes
Test your knowledge.

Embedded Weblinks
Gain additional information for research.

Slide Show
View images and captions, and prepare a presentation.

Try This!
Complete activities and hands-on experiments.

... and much, much more!

Go to **www.av2books.com**, and enter this book's unique code.

BOOK CODE

C 3 0 4 4 4 5

AV² by Weigl brings you media enhanced books that support active learning.

Published by AV² by Weigl
350 5th Avenue, 59th Floor
New York, NY 10118
Website: www.av2books.com   www.weigl.com

Library of Congress Cataloging-in-Publication Data

Yasuda, Anita.
 Foxes / Anita Yasuda.
     p. cm. -- (Backyard animals)
 Includes index.
 ISBN 978-1-61690-620-7 (hardcover : alk. paper) -- ISBN 978-1-61690-626-9 (softcover : alk. paper)
 1. Foxes--Juvenile literature. I. Title.
 QL737.C22Y37 2011
 599.775--dc22

                                     2010046086

Printed in the United States of America in North Mankato, Minnesota
1 2 3 4 5 6 7 8 9 0 15 14 13 12 11

052011
WEP37500

Editor Jordan McGill   **Design** Terry Paulhus

Every reasonable effort has been made to trace ownership and to obtain permission to reprint copyright material. The publishers would be pleased to have any errors or omissions brought to their attention so that they may be corrected in subsequent printings.

Photo Credits
Weigl acknowledges Getty Images as its primary photo supplier for this title.

Contents

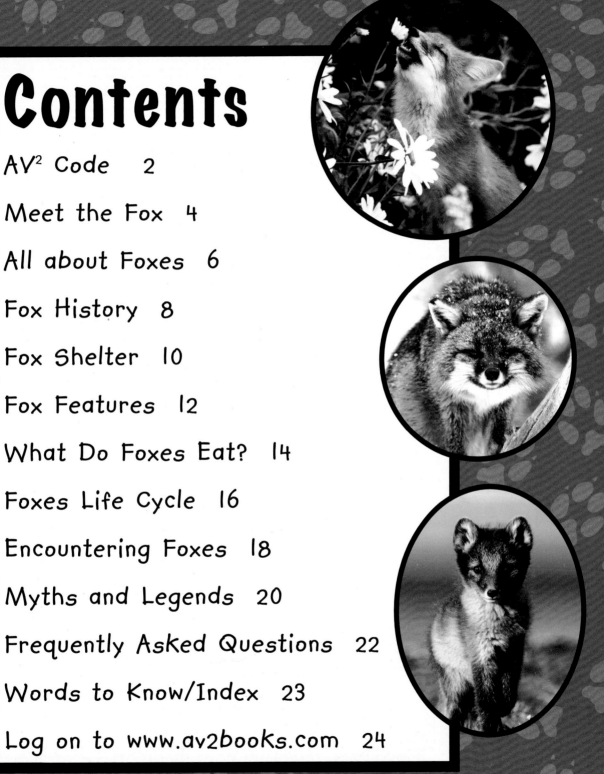

Meet the Fox

Foxes are **mammals**. They have slender bodies that are covered in long fur. Their tails are bushy, and their muzzles are narrow. Some foxes have large, pointy ears.

Foxes live in nearly every part of the world. They roam Arctic **tundras** and African deserts. They live in marshes, grasslands, and mountains. Many foxes make their homes in towns and cities.

Foxes come in many colors. Their fur may be red, brown, black, silver, gray, or white. Some foxes are as large as a medium-sized dog. Others are as small as a house cat.

Fascinating Facts

Foxes communicate through sounds and actions. Sometimes, they make a loud bark, squeal, or howl that is similar to a human scream.

Most dogs hunt in groups called packs. The fox is like a cat. It hunts alone.

All about Foxes

There are 10 **species** of fox. Six species of fox live in North America. These are the red, gray, Arctic, kit, swift, and island fox.

Foxes are a member of the *Canidae*, or dog family. Wolves, coyotes, jackals, and dogs are cousins of the fox.

The two most common fox species in North America are the red fox and the gray fox. The red fox is the longest fox, at 20 to 30 inches (50 to 75 centimeters). The gray fox is **native** to North America. Adult gray foxes weigh about 7 to 13 pounds (3 to 6 kg).

The gray fox is the only member of the dog family that can climb trees.

Where Foxes Live

Red Fox

Found in North America, Europe, Asia, North Africa, and Australia

Fennec Fox

Lives in northern Africa

Swift Fox

Resides in the plains of North America

Arctic Fox

Resides in the Arctic regions of Eurasia, North America, and Iceland

Fox History

Fossils of ancient dogs date back 40 to 50 million years. These animals looked like a mix between a fox and a weasel. Scientists believe that an **ancestor** of the fox lived about 3.5 million years ago.

The oldest fossil remains of foxes in North America belong to the gray fox. These fossils are 1.5 million years old. The species is thought to have come from North America before it traveled south into Central and South America.

The red fox was brought by settlers to North America from Europe in the 17th century. Settlers introduced the red fox to Australia and New Zealand in the mid-19th century.

Fascinating Facts

Even though foxes are considered part of the dog family, they have claws and eyes that are similar to those of a cat.

Some species of fox have fur that changes color in winter. The Arctic fox's fur changes from brown to white.

Fox Shelter

Foxes make **dens** in caves, fallen logs, or under deep brush. They also move into dens that rabbits or marmots once used. Foxes line their dens with grass and leaves. This keeps the den warm. Some fox dens have up to 100 entrances. This allows a fox to escape in case of danger.

Arctic foxes often make dens on the sides of hills or cliffs because the ground is too hard. In harsh weather, such as strong blizzards, Arctic foxes will bury themselves in the snow for protection.

In warm weather, foxes sleep outdoors. They wrap their tail around themselves to keep warm.

Some foxes make their dens in abandoned buzzard nests.

Arctic foxes can survive temperatures as low as -94 degrees Fahrenheit (-70 degrees Celsius).

Fox Features

Foxes use their fur to keep warm during winter months. In autumn, some foxes grow more fur to prepare for winter. The color of the fur they grow for winter matches their surroundings. This keeps them hidden from **predators**. In spring, foxes shed their extra fur. During summer months, short fur protects foxes from the Sun's heat.

TAIL
A fox's tail is also known as a brush or sweep. It is one-third of their body length. The tail is used for balance and to communicate with other foxes. A raised tail might show that the fox is confident.

PAWS
Once a fox captures its **prey**, it uses its paws to hold it down. A fox also uses its paws to dig holes.

EARS

Foxes have large ears and good hearing. They can hear a small mammal move underground. A fox will dig through dirt or snow to catch prey that it hears beneath the ground.

EYES

Foxes have large, dark eyes with oval pupils. They have excellent vision, especially in the dark. Foxes will remain motionless until they notice the smallest movement of their prey. Then, they quickly pounce.

MUZZLE

Foxes have a slender nose. It is very sensitive to smell. Foxes use their excellent sense of smell to find prey. They also use it to sense danger by smell.

LEGS

Foxes have strong legs. This allows them to reach speeds of 30 miles (48 kilometers) per hour. A fox can jump over obstacles as high as 7 feet (2 meters).

What Do Foxes Eat?

Foxes are omnivores. Omnivores are mammals that eat both plants and animals. Foxes eat rabbits, birds, fish, and **invertebrates** such as insects, mollusks, earthworms, and crayfish. They also eat fruit, such as blueberries, apples, and plums.

Foxes often hunt for food from sunset until the early morning. A red fox may travel up to 5 miles (8 km) in one night looking for food.

A cache is a shallow hole in the ground where a fox stores its food. Foxes often eat the food soon after storing it, usually the next day.

The bat-eared fox of Africa eats termites. It licks them from the ground. This fox can eat over one million termites each year.

Young foxes play by sneaking up on and surprising each other. They do this to practice hunting.

Foxes Life Cycle

Foxes **mate** once a year, in winter. Female foxes give off a scent that lets male foxes know they are ready to mate.

Birth

A baby fox is called a pup, or cub. At birth, it weighs less than 2 ounces (57 grams). That is about the same weight as a stick of butter. A baby fox's eyes are closed tight when it is born. The pup is blind, deaf, and toothless. Most often, there are 1 to 10 pups born in each **litter**. Pups drink milk from their mother for their first month of life.

Two to Four Weeks

At two weeks, the pup's eyes open. By one month, they have their first teeth and can eat food that has been chewed by their mother. The pups are able to go outside the den. The parents watch for predators such as coyotes or wolves.

The female fox gives birth after 51 to 57 days. The baby foxes are born in the den. Both parents raise the young.

Six to Eight Weeks

Pups stop drinking their mother's milk after six weeks. They can eat solid food. The father brings his pups live prey to eat.

Seven Months to One Year

A fox is fully grown by the time it is seven months old. By then, it has learned how to find and catch food. By fall, foxes are ready to leave the den. Foxes live about three to five years. Some foxes live as long as 12 years.

Encountering Foxes

Foxes are mainly **nocturnal**. When the sun sets, they search for food. Sometimes, foxes can be seen in the daytime near their dens or lying in deep brush. Foxes like to dig in gardens for grubs, earthworms, and beetles.

Foxes rarely approach humans. It is important to stay away from a fox if one is seen in nature. Foxes have sharp teeth and claws, and they may bite. They can also carry diseases, such as **rabies**.

People should never feed a fox. It may become used to human food and return for more. To keep foxes from coming around homes, people should properly dispose of all garbage in a sealed can.

In some parts of the world, foxes are hunted for their fur.

It is important to dispose of garbage in sealed containers and bring pet food indoors. Foxes will eat garbage and pet food left outside.

Myths and Legends

In Great Britain during the **Middle Ages**, seeing a black fox was thought to be unlucky. It was a symbol of disaster.

India, China, Korea, and Japan all have tales of fox spirits. In Japanese legends, the fox is a creature with magical abilities. It is able to take on human form. The fox is also thought to be the messenger of Inari, the god of rice and food. Fox statues can be seen in Japan guarding some **Shinto** shrines. In Japan, the fox is considered a **sacred** animal.

In German fairy tales, the fox is a mischievous character who tricks other animals into giving up their food.

The Fox and the Crow

Aesop was an ancient Greek storyteller. This is one of his tales about a fox. It tells how one should not trust people who are overly kind.

One day, Fox saw Crow fly off with a chunk of cheese in her mouth. Fox wanted the cheese, so he thought of a plan to get it. Fox waited until Crow landed in a nearby tree and went to greet her.

"Good morning, Miss Crow," he said. "Your feathers look lovely today."

Crow was happy with the kind words, so Fox continued. "Your voice is the sweetest in the land. If I could only hear you sing once, I would call you queen of the birds."

Crow was happy to sing. As she opened her mouth, the cheese fell into Fox's paw.

"Thank you," said Fox. "This is all I really wanted. In the future Miss Crow, do not trust **flatterers**."

Frequently Asked Questions

How does an Arctic fox stay warm?

Answer: The Arctic fox has **adapted** to cold weather. The fox's thick fur helps it survive in extreme cold. Hair on the fox's foot pads keeps the animal from freezing and slipping on the ice.

Do foxes have predators?

Answer: Foxes have many predators. They include coyotes, hawks, eagles, owls, bears, mountain lions, and humans.

Why do red foxes make human-like screams?

Answer: Foxes make sounds to communicate with other members of their family. They also make sounds to drive away intruders.

Words to Know

adapted: adjusted to the natural environment

ancestor: a person, plant, or animal from a past time

dens: places where foxes live, such as a hollow, cave, or a log

flatterers: people who say nice things to make others like them

fossils: traces of an animal that are left behind in rocks

invertebrates: animals that have no backbone

litter: a group of pups born together

mammals: animals that have fur, make milk, and are born live

mate: breed

Middle Ages: a period from A.D. 500 to 1453

native: original to the area

nocturnal: animals that are active at night

predators: animals that hunt other animals for food

prey: an animal that is hunted or caught for food

rabies: a disease that can be passed between animals and humans

sacred: respected due to tradition

Shinto: a Japanese religion

species: a group of similar animals that can mate together

tundras: flat, treeless places where the ground remains frozen all year

Index

Log on to www.av2books.com

AV² by Weigl brings you media enhanced books that support active learning. Go to www.av2books.com, and enter the special code found on page 2 of this book. You will gain access to enriched and enhanced content that supplements and complements this book. Content includes video, audio, web links, quizzes, a slide show, and activities.

Audio
Listen to sections of the book read aloud.

Video
Watch informative video clips.

Embedded Weblinks
Gain additional information for research.

Try This!
Complete activities and hands-on experiments.

WHAT'S ONLINE?

Try This!	Embedded Weblinks	Video	**EXTRA FEATURES**
Identify different types of foxes.	More information on identification.	Watch a video about fox behavior.	
List important features of the fox.	More information on the history of foxes.	See a fox in its natural environment.	
Compare the similarities and differences between young and adult foxes.	Complete an interactive activity.		
Test your knowledge of foxes.	More information on encountering foxes.		
	More stories and legends.		

Audio
Listen to sections of the book read aloud.

Key Words
Study vocabulary, and complete a matching word activity.

Slide Show
View images and captions, and prepare a presentation.

Quizzes
Test your knowledge.

AV² was built to bridge the gap between print and digital. We encourage you to tell us what you like and what you want to see in the future.

Sign up to be an AV² Ambassador at www.av2books.com/ambassador.